THE FACILITATOR'S POCKETBOOK

By John Townsend & Paul Donovan
Drawings by Phil Hailstone

"John and Paul provide a quick route to a practical understanding of facilitation. This book should be compulsory reading for all managers handling change."
Teresa Kilmartin, Executive Manager Training & Development, Irish Life Assurance plc

"This book is the perfect illustration of what facilitation is all about – making things easy. Reflecting on the methods, skills and techniques described, it is easy to understand what it takes to become a skilled facilitator. Read it and you will undoubtedly do it better and get better results!"
Karin Priarollo, Director, Human Resources, Novartis Consumer Health

CONTENTS

INTRODUCTION 1
Definition, typical situations, the facilitator's role

PLANNING THE FACILITATION SESSION 5
Session objective, ground rules, focus question, discussion question, process, vernissage, participants

FACILITATION METHODS 13
Facilitraining rainbow, process monitoring, brainstorming, facilitating discussion, Socratic direction, teaching, demonstrating, presenting

SESSION SKILLS 23
Setting the scene, stimulating interest, valorising participants, seeking consensus, provoking controversy, essential and non-essential contributions, recognising commonality, revitalising the group, orienting the group to action, summarising

INTERPERSONAL SKILLS 33
Questioning, listening, giving feedback, conflict handling

ENERGISERS 45
Look back, bodyguards and assassins, a pat on the back

PROBLEM-SOLVING/REFRAMING 51
TECHNIQUES
Brainstorming, talking wall, columns/clusters, pluses and minuses, role debate, critical mass, 2005, greenfield site, transporter, force field analysis, must have/nice to have, time beam, eureka

HELPFUL ATTITUDES AND VALUES 67
My mind-set won't help them, unconditional positive regard, OK to teach, no one best way, people never argue with their own data, facilitators can't win arguments, silence is OK, don't push the river

THE KNOWLEDGE BASE 77
Learning styles, four phases of team development, NLP, dissonance and self-justification, locus of control, unfreeze-move-refreeze, bases of power, definitions of organisational development and culture, self-fulfilling prophecy

REFERENCES & FURTHER READING 88

1 INTRODUCTION

DEFINITION OF FACILITATION

Literally, facilitation means 'making things easy'.

In today's workplaces, facilitators make things easier by:

Using a range of skills and methods to bring the best out in people as they work to achieve results in interactive events.

Typically, facilitators are asked to help people to make decisions and achieve results in meetings, teambuilding sessions, problem-solving groups and training events.

TYPICAL FACILITATION SITUATIONS

- A senior line manager asks you to 'lead' a meeting, by the end of which he wants to have his team reach consensus on the best way of co-ordinating a complex process

- A project manager is having difficulty getting a temporary cross-functional project team off the ground and asks you to come in and help them to organise themselves

- The training manager invites you to come and 'facilitate' an introductory module on the New Hires Programme

- A team leader calls you in to facilitate a session with her team where she's expecting a conflict to occur between two volatile team members and doesn't know how to handle it

- A conference organiser hires you to facilitate a break-out session with 50 delegates

- The marketing manager asks you to lead a creative brainstorming session on new products

THE FACILITATOR'S ROLE

- **Generalist and Specialist**
  - general knowledge of how organisations function and specialised knowledge of organisational diagrams and intervention processes.

- **Co-ordinator**
  - the link between the client and the group. The organiser of resources and expertise.

- **Neutral Observer**
  - belonging to no political coalition within an organisation and being seen as having no stake in any outcome.

  Adapted from Beer (1980)

Facilitators have to be able to cope with uncertainty, knowing that things may not turn out as predicted or hoped for. They must be able to use the power of their credibility to help people address issues. They need to be calm in times of emotion when others are stressed and confused.

Facilitators need to be able to empathise with people and listen well. They need to be able to support and counsel others who may be having a hard time in the session; to describe in understandable ways the processes and systems they are proposing; to mobilise energy in self and client; to surface difficult issues and help others to do so; to take themselves less seriously and more humorously.

PLANNING THE FACILITATION SESSION

PLANNING THE FACILITATION SESSION

1. THE SESSION OBJECTIVE

Whatever the topic and whoever the participants, the first step for the facilitator is to define clearly the objective of the session. What, specifically, do you/the client want to have achieved as a result of the session?

Example:
By the end of the session we will have established
an action plan for improving our team meetings.

In some cases (eg: 'improving the quality of our
leadership') it may be necessary to get the group to
agree on a clear definition of the topic before launching
the session.

2. THE GROUND RULES

As soon as you have announced or agreed upon an overall objective for the session, it's vital to establish and get the group's total agreement on some behavioural and/or administrative ground rules.

These might include:

- Being 'tough on the problems but not on the people'
- Asking for everyone's opinion in turn
- Appointing a scribe or notetaker
- Limiting the amount of time each person can speak
- Not interrupting one another, etc

These rules will help you stay on track during the discussions – especially if conflict arises!

3. THE FOCUS QUESTION

The focus question is a powerful visual means to test 'buy in' from all participants at the beginning of a session. It focuses their attention by getting them to commit themselves as to whether or not this **is** an important issue for them. You should **plan** it only after you have decided on the Discussion Question (Step 4) but **ask** it as Step 3 in the session sequence.

Like all agreed process items, it allows you, as the facilitator, to come back later if you need to keep things on track. A useful way to introduce the focus question is to provide a scale from low to high and ask participants to rate 'to what extent ...?' or 'how important ...?' with adhesive dots or marks on the scale.

Example:
'To what extent are effective meetings important to the success of our team?'

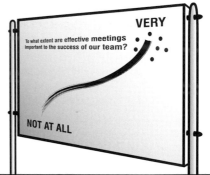

4. THE DISCUSSION QUESTION

The quality of the information you gather with this process is only as good as the discussion question. It should ask for **details of the problem** and **not** solutions.

Example:
'What's wrong with our team meetings?'

If solutions are requested at this stage (ie: 'How could we **improve** our meetings?') some major components of a problem might be missed.

5. THE PROCESS

In this pocketbook we outline a number of processes/techniques for helping groups solve a problem and there are many more.

As a professional facilitator you will plan to use what you consider to be the most appropriate process, given the data you are likely to get from the discussion question. See the chapter on problem-solving and reframing for a description of some powerful processes to add to your toolkit.

6. VERNISSAGE

Instead of presenting the results of their group work, teams visit the Action Plan board of other teams (like at a 'vernissage' on the first day of an exhibition at a gallery). Each participant has three possible ways of commenting **silently** on the work of his/her colleagues:

 Writing/sticking a heart shape to show agreement with any point and adding a comment which builds on that point

 Writing/sticking a 'lightning' flash to indicate disagreement with any point and adding a reason for disagreement

 Writing/sticking a question mark to say 'I don't understand this point'

You, as a facilitator, then lead the final discussion to clarify all the vernissage hearts, flashes and question marks.

7. THE PARTICIPANTS

Although it's not always possible to know very much about the people who are going to participate in the session, **any** prior information will help you do a better job.

- Do any of them have a vested interest in a particular outcome?

- Are any of them under pressure to argue for a certain solution?

- Have any feathers been ruffled recently by organisational decisions?

- Has past experience shown that certain people tend to act in certain ways during such sessions?

- To what extent will participants' personalities affect the way you run the session?

- Will participants' 'rank' mean that you'll need special ground rules?

Proper planning will mean that you make a list of the participants and note down anything you know which might affect the process or outcome.

FACILITATION METHODS

FACILITATION METHODS

THE FACILITRAINING RAINBOW

The two key ingredients in any facilitation/training intervention are:
1. How much interaction does the facilitator have with participants?
2. How much does the facilitator contribute to the content/outcome of the session?
All 'facilitraining' interventions are a mixture of these two ingredients.

Here is a way of deciding which method to use and when. Using the criteria on the chart under the rainbow (and any others you want to add) simply score the session on the billiard-type sliding scales.

Examples:
- How much time will you have for the session? The less time available, the more likely you are to have to contribute more yourself and interact less with participants.
- What is participants' present knowledge of the subject? The more they know the more you just facilitate the process.
- What do participants expect from the session – to be told what to do, to discuss or to decide? Depending on the organisational/geographical culture you may start by presenting and only move to process monitoring later in the session.

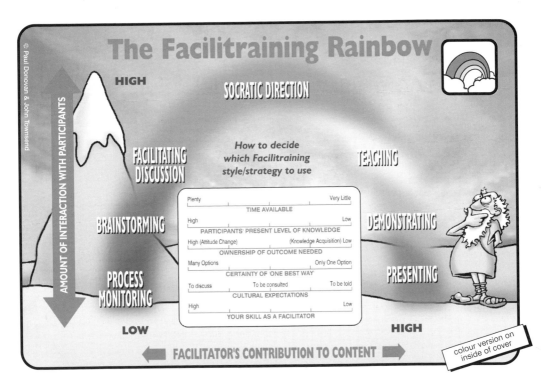

PROCESS MONITORING

(Low interaction/low contribution)

As the 'guardian of the process', the facilitator makes no personal contribution to the content of the discussion but occasionally regulates the flow of participants' contributions, according to a previously agreed set of process rules.

BRAINSTORMING

(Low to medium interaction/low contribution)

Here the facilitator 'conducts' a classic brainstorming session – interacting with participants only to encourage them to give their ideas, but hardly ever evaluating or adding ideas.

FACILITATING DISCUSSION

(Medium to high interaction/low to medium contribution)

When using this style the facilitator interacts quite often with participants to invite opinions, control the process and give own opinions (if only to provoke more discussion).

SOCRATIC DIRECTION

(High interaction/medium to high contribution)

This is the method pioneered by Socrates whereby the facilitator asks questions and then reformulates the answers as necessary to lead participants to a desired learning outcome. The rainbow provides for a wide range of leading strategies – from relatively open to relatively closed.

The common element in all Socratic strategies is the high amount of interaction. It is based on the premise that people don't argue with their own data, even when it is massaged and channelled towards a 'hidden' learning outcome – as long as the 'facipulation' is done professionally and sincerely.

SOCRATIC DIRECTION

FACILITATION METHODS

TEACHING

(Medium to high interaction/medium to high contribution)

When, in the classic teaching mode, the facilitator provides structured learning experiences and guides participants towards pre-determined learning objectives. He or she, nevertheless, allows some latitude for interpretation at an individual level.

TEACHING

FACILITATION METHODS

DEMONSTRATING

(Medium to low interaction/high contribution)

Not as 'one-way' as lecturing, demonstration involves interaction with participants, in as much as they are asked to try out in some way what has been presented.

FACILITATION METHODS

PRESENTING

(Low interaction/high contribution)

The classical and often vital style needed to put across information.

However, as competition from the multimedia environment grows, trainers need to perform at an increasingly professional pitch to stop being 'zapped', or tuned out, by participants!

SESSION SKILLS

SETTING THE SCENE

The first skill needed by a facilitator in any situation is that of making people feel that they are welcome and in good hands. You demonstrate this skill when you:

- Engage in useful small talk
- Build rapport by linking to participants' experiences
- Describe objectives in a way that appeals to everyone
- Establish credibility by connecting to participants' concerns/jargon, etc

SESSION SKILLS

STIMULATING INTEREST & CURIOSITY

Facilitation means making it easy for people to discuss and decide. They will only discuss and decide if they are motivated to do so. This means that a good facilitator will:

- Phrase discussion and focus questions that are inviting
  (see pages 8 and 9)
- Supply attractive processes with which to analyse and solve problems
  (see pages 51 to 66)

VALORISING PARTICIPANTS

In all participant-led facilitation sessions a key skill is to make the attendees all feel **valued**. This is what we mean by 'valorise'.

In order to accomplish this, the facilitator must:

- Adopt 'unconditional positive regard' for all participants – it's **their** session after all
- Boost quieter individuals' confidence by encouraging their contributions
- Build on people's suggestions
- Banter with extroverts

SEEKING CONSENSUS

Consensus is not when everyone agrees but when they agree to agree! In order to help a group reach consensus, the professional facilitator will:

- Identify points of agreement
- Reformulate contributions to highlight common ideas
- Explore people's objectives
- Encourage people to build on others' ideas
- Test false consensus due to conformity (is agreement real?)
- Test consensus for relevance to objective
- Test consensus for underlying motivation (is agreement biased in any way?)

PROVOKING USEFUL CONTROVERSY

Philosophers refer to 'Thesis/Antithesis/Synthesis'. Useful controversy means looking at both sides of a problem before deciding what to do. Professional facilitators do this when they:

- Phrase challenging questions (see page 34)
- Supply 'reframing' and/or creative problem-solving techniques (see pages 51 to 66)

They will also be skilled at dealing with the inevitable conflict which controversy brings and will:

- Reassert agreed ground rules on interpersonal behaviour

- Help the group 'be tough on the problem but not on the people'

DISTINGUISHING BETWEEN ESSENTIAL & NON-ESSENTIAL CONTRIBUTIONS

This is one of the most important and yet the most difficult facilitation skills. It's obviously easier when the facilitator knows the participants and their problem inside out. However, this is often not the case. In fact, it's more often the opposite. The facilitator is called in precisely because he or she does not know the content/subject matter and can, therefore, remain neutral. So we must:

- Constantly relate contributions to session objectives

- Monitor participants' body language for significant reactions to contributions and to people (What do **they** seem to think is essential? Whom do **they** seem to take most seriously during discussions?)

- Monitor group behaviour for clues to organisational pressure on decisions (What do **they** seem to think is important for the organisation? Whom do they listen to/agree with most?)

RECOGNISING COMMONALITIES, THEMES & TRENDS

The whole idea of facilitation is to build on common ground, to build consensus, to build decisions. A key skill for this is to recognise what **is** common ground. Experience is the best teacher here so, when in doubt as to whether there is commonality:

- Explore people's intentions and key concerns by asking for clarification to help your growing hypotheses

- Listen for frequently used words and phrases from different people which imply that consensus is building (or not!)

REVITALISING THE GROUP

From time to time even the best facilitated sessions run out of steam. A good facilitator will recognise these dips instantly and react quickly to:

- Supply energisers (see pages 45-50)
- Refocus on the value of the discussion
- Bring people into the discussion who seem to be drifting
- Engage people who had useful contributions earlier but maybe now think they have nothing to add

ORIENTING THE GROUP TO ACTION

Too many facilitation sessions end when everyone 'feels good' rather than when a decision has been made. Since the objective of any facilitation session is to reach an objective, the facilitator will:

- Brainstorm action options
- Supply useful prioritisation techniques
- Supply decision-making methods
- Help the group to phrase decisions
- Assist in allocating tasks and responsibilities

Summarising

At the end of every session a good facilitator will:

- Recap the chronology of the session
- Highlight the key consensus items
- Reiterate the action plan

1 INTERPERSONAL SKILLS

QUESTIONING

The ability to ask good questions is vital to the success of a facilitator. But the information you get is only as good as the questions you ask.

Closed questions (those which only have one answer)
Sometimes it's necessary to collect concrete information from a group and a good closed questioning technique will help you do this efficiently. **'Who, what, when, where?'** questions will get you tight information and, if you add words like 'specifically?' and 'exactly?' to your question, you'll help people to be even more precise.

Open questions (those which have many answers)
At all stages of a facilitation, open questions ensure open discussions.

Examples:
'Tell me **about**...'
'**How** do you feel when...?'
'**Why** do you think this happened?'
'**What** would you do **if**...'

INTERPERSONAL SKILLS

LISTENING

As a facilitator, in order to listen you have to talk!

That is, you have to show you're listening. And the way to show you're listening is to ask reflective questions or 'reformulate' what you think you heard someone saying. This **active** listening process is vital to the smooth running of any facilitation process. It's probably **the** key skill for any facilitator.

Good listening means concentrating hard on the whole message from someone:

- Watching their body language for congruence with the message they're giving
- Listening to the kinds of words they're using; trying to understand where they're coming from as they speak
- Checking growing hypotheses about how what they're saying fits with the discussion so far
- Resisting temptation to double guess without reflecting back what you think you're hearing

GIVING FEEDBACK 1

Giving feedback can be an important part of some facilitation sessions – especially those contained within a training programme.

There is no doubt that people improve and grow most when they receive sincere feedback on what they do well, and are given constructive help to find ways of overcoming barriers to their effectiveness.

Whenever you are asked to facilitate giving feedback to a group or to individuals, help them to think through these three questions:

1. **What did you do well?**
2. **What could you have done even better?**
3. **What prevented you from doing even better; what's the plan to do even better in the future?**

GIVING FEEDBACK 2

THE WIZARD OF OZ FACTOR

Like the Wizard of Oz who conferred his gifts upon the Tin Man, the Lion and the Scarecrow, we should affirm people into greatness! Often, because of our lack of line authority, we underestimate what a powerful force for personal growth we can be.

If we can show people a picture of themselves as successful and competent, then they have a much greater chance of becoming successful and competent than if we confirm their present negative self-image. Let's concentrate on the things they have done well, estimate their potential in that area, and then give feedback to them as if they have already achieved success.

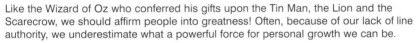

- Build on their strengths

- Give them heart and courage; make them feel intelligent and powerful

- Show them how to feel ten feet tall and then they will be ready to take to the yellow brick road!

INTERPERSONAL SKILLS

CONFLICT HANDLING

PLEASE REFER BACK TO THE FACILITRAINING RAINBOW ON P.15

If conflict emerges during process monitoring, brainstorming, facilitating discussion or participant-led Socratic direction it tends to involve two or more of the **participants**

If conflict emerges while presenting, demonstrating, teaching or *leading* a Socratic direction session, it tends to involve the **facilitator** and one or more of the **participants**

SOCRATIC DIRECTION

FACILITATING DISCUSSION

TEACHING

BRAINSTORMING

DEMONSTRATING

PROCESS MONITORING

PRESENTING

CONFLICT may emerge in the form of disagreement with:
• The message • The sponsor • The process • The facilitator • One or more of the participants

38

CONFLICT HANDLING WHEN PRESENTING

When a participant raises objections or
'heckles':

AFFIRM your position.
Restate your case.
Draw on new arguments to convince.

AVOID
Ignore the interruption.
Say you will handle questions later.
Ask for questioners to 'park' their
objections on a board.

CONFLICT HANDLING WHEN DEMONSTRATING

When a participant raises objections or disagrees:

POSTPONE

Ask them to hold their thoughts until after the demo.

DEBATE

Enter a brief discussion to argue your point.
Support with examples.
Introduce new elements into the demo.

INTERPERSONAL SKILLS

CONFLICT HANDLING WHEN TEACHING

When a participant raises objections or disagrees:

AGREE on minor points and accommodate their views in your teaching.

DISCUSS briefly the merits of the objection but reaffirm your position.

SHELVE items causing conflict until later.

CONFLICT HANDLING WHEN IN SOCRATIC DIRECTION

When a participant raises objections or disagrees:

REFLECT/DEFLECT
Reflect back what you think you heard.
Deflect to others for their views.

QUESTION
Ask questions to help the objector
explore his or her views in more depth.

COLLABORATE
Recognise the objection and ask the group to
include it in the session outcome/results.

When two or more participants are in conflict:
LEAD
Identify the 'correct' position and influence
the group to accept it.

INTERPERSONAL SKILLS

CONFLICT HANDLING WHEN FACILITATING DISCUSSION

When two or more participants are in conflict, help them to either:

HOLD their disagreement until later.

COMPROMISE by 'splitting the difference'.

COLLABORATE by seeking out a win/win solution.

FACILITATING DISCUSSION

RMING

CONFLICT HANDLING WHEN BRAINSTORMING/PROCESS MONITORING

When two or more participants are in conflict when **brainstorming**:

RESTATE the ground rules to which they **all** previously agreed (see page 7).

When two or more participants are in conflict when **process monitoring**:

MIRROR

Use non-judgemental reflective statements which help the whole group see what's happening and take action.

ENERGISERS

LIFTING ENERGY LEVELS

One of the key session skills which facilitators need is to supply and animate energisers. However well your session is running, there's always going to be a moment when enthusiasm and energy drop. That's when you need an energiser!

On the next four pages are examples of tried and tested ways of lifting lagging energy and reviving enthusiasm in an otherwise productive group. You can use them when you get an after-lunch dip in concentration, a morning need for a wake-up activity or a sudden requirement to shift gears, change subjects or smooth over a smouldering conflict.

LOOK BACK

When the group is feeling a little tired and fed up, take a break, and when you come back conduct a 'look back' exercise over what has been achieved already. But this should be done using unusual media or methods which have not already been used during the facilitation to date.

For example, groups could produce a montage of their achievement on the wall using available materials. Or they could make a summary using markers on a cheap white T-shirt. Others could draw a map representing progress to date. Another group could perform a mime which would illustrate the course of the facilitation so far.

By using a light-hearted touch the facilitator can help produce a feeling of playfulness and energy in the group to help them move on to the next phase (and to celebrate what has already been achieved).

BODYGUARDS & ASSASSINS

This is a quick and devastatingly effective energiser which has been around for some time.

First, you ask every participant silently to pick one of the people in the room as a possible bodyguard, someone they think could protect them if need be.

Then ask them to pick an assassin. Someone who, for the purposes of the exercise, they choose to be in fear of.

Once each person has mentally decided on who's who, you announce that they are to spend three minutes (without speaking a word) moving as far away as possible from their 'assassin' and as close as possible to their bodyguard.

It doesn't take much imagination to picture how this one works!

A PAT ON THE BACK

Just before everyone goes home after a long and tiring session ask your participants to form a close circle and to turn to their right. Then each one should give the person in front of them a pat on the back in recognition of a job well done!

This energiser, made famous in Alan Parker's film, The Commitments, is a simple way to get people to recognise that they have achieved something to be proud of during the day.

NOTES

PROBLEM-SOLVING/
REFRAMING TECHNIQUES

PROBLEM-SOLVING/REFRAMING TECHNIQUES

BRAINSTORMING

When in doubt about which technique to use, you can always fall back on brainstorming! Here's a reminder of the basic rules:

- Working with a flip chart/pinboard, ask each member in turn to suggest a solution to the problem

- Record **all** ideas on the flip chart and number them to ease final selection

- Encourage and provoke participants to give ideas or pass; after two have 'passed', switch to popcorn mode where anyone can call out an idea as it comes – 'crazy' and 'stupid' ideas should be encouraged as well as those which 'piggyback' on others

- Proceed until ideas dry up, then give each participant five votes to distribute to the ideas (except their own!) in any way they wish

THE TALKING WALL

Clouds

Write directly on to large sheets of brown recycled paper

Post-Its A5

Hexagons (for clustering)

Standard

Pinboard Cards (for categories)

Why not use a flip chart as a Talking Wall?

The ideal, time-saving method for brainstorming, problem-solving and discussion leading.

- Allows EVERYONE to participate
- Encourages creative thinking
- Gives an OVERVIEW to all
- Facilitates immediate clustering and categorising

Thumb Tacks

MARKER

Voting Dots

GLUE STICK

SPRAY

Post-its: standard or specially made. Quick and easy

53

PROBLEM-SOLVING/REFRAMING TECHNIQUES

COLUMNS/CLUSTERS

A: INFORMATION GATHERING

- Distribute cards/post-it notes to individuals, pairs or trios. Ask them to write **one** answer to the discussion question (see page 9) on each card (no more than five words per card).

- Collect cards and stick on the pinboard/flip chart either in columns or in clusters as follows:

  - **Columns:** Mix/shuffle cards and read them one by one asking: 'existing or new column?'. Wait till the group agrees before sticking them in columns. In case of disagreement, let the card initiator decide.

  - **Clusters:** Ask participants to stick their cards at random onto the pinboard/flip chart as soon as they are ready. Get them to eliminate duplicates and cluster them in categories of similarity.

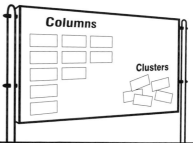

COLUMNS/CLUSTERS

B: CATEGORISING & CHOOSING

Brainstorm with the group the best heading for each column/cluster category (maximum three words), write it on a new, different coloured card and stick it on top of each column or cluster.

a) First copy all the category headings onto a new, pre-prepared pinboard/flip chart with five columns (see drawing) for:
  ● Category heading ● Names of participants ● Voting dots ● Score ● Ranking

b) Next, give adhesive voting dots to each participant (as many dots as the number of categories divided by two, plus one extra). Ask them to allocate their votes in any way they wish.

c) Count the number of dots for each category. Write the total in the score column. Rank the top three or the top five.

d) Ask participants to write their names on cards/post-it notes and to stick them in column 2 against the category they wish to work on. Equalise the group numbers by asking the stragglers or the undecided to change/join groups.

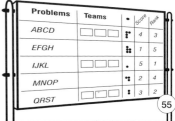

Problems	Teams	•	Score	Rank
ABCD	☐☐☐	⁚•	4	3
EFGH		⁝⁝	1	5
IJKL	☐☐☐	•	5	1
MNOP		•⁝	2	4
QRST	☐☐☐	⁚	3	2

55

PLUSES, MINUSES & INTERESTING FACTS

This technique was developed by Edward de Bono as a way of getting people to consider all aspects of a situation – the advantages, disadvantages and other incidental issues which emerge, such as new opportunities previously unseen.

It's useful if a group is fairly antagonistic to a proposal or change.

Divide the board into three sections (pluses, minuses, interesting facts) and ask three small groups each to work on one of the sections. They bring back their findings on stickies, and post them on the board/present them to the others.

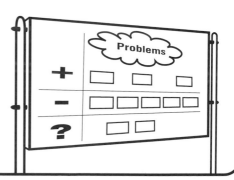

PROBLEM-SOLVING/REFRAMING TECHNIQUES

ROLE DEBATE

Create a case study on a controversial issue and oblige strong-minded people to take views which are different from their own.

Switching roles regularly will get participants to exercise their minds around new attitudes and opinions.

As Abraham Lincoln said:
"A mind once stretched by an idea never returns to the same shape.".

57

CRITICAL MASS

Who are the people who must be convinced in order for change to take place?

The change becomes less daunting when people realise that you do not have to convince everyone about change - only the leaders of opinion. The rest will follow.

Ask groups to name them and report on how they plan to recruit them to the cause in plenary.

PROBLEM-SOLVING/REFRAMING TECHNIQUES

2010

It is now 2010 and all of our dreams have been achieved. Every business plan has been fulfilled and the mission is a reality. Now step back and describe how we did it!

What happened in between to make our dream a reality? Use the past tense.

This technique is very useful when the group has low morale or when the barriers to change seem insurmountable.

Break into subgroups and ask each one to present their 'how we did it' story in plenary.

BUSINESS PLAN ACHIEVED

PROBLEM-SOLVING/REFRAMING TECHNIQUES

GREENFIELD SITE

What would we do if we had no history, rules, regulations, culture or climate? If none of these things existed because we were just starting up, then how would we approach the problem?

This is a useful technique when a group is hampered by culture, habit or other restrictions.

Get small groups to imagine the consequences of these scenarios and to present their findings in plenary.

TRANSPORTER

How would they tackle this issue in ...(Intel, HP, Volvo, Japan, USA, Malaysia?)

This is useful for abandoning traditional modes of thought or for getting free from culture for a short time.

Ask groups to work on the problem as if they were XYZ and report back in plenary.

FORCE FIELD ANALYSIS

Working from the problem, write the '**desired state**' on the board and then divide the board into two halves.

The left side represents all the forces which are working against reaching the desired state and the right side those forces which are pushing towards reaching it. Get team members to suggest negative and positive forces. Each should be agreed with the team before being displayed (on cards/post-it notes or written directly on board) and perhaps **weighted**.

Turn the board around and make a summary of the **action steps** needed to support the positive and restrain the negative forces.

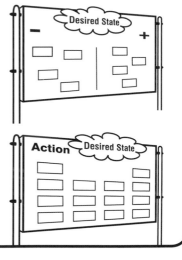

MUST HAVE/NICE TO HAVE

In decision-making, sometimes a group becomes obsessed with democracy, allowing each suggestion to have equal weight and air time. This is why so many 'camels' are created by committees who start out trying to invent a horse.

'Must have/nice to have' is a technique to use **after** the group has surfaced a number of solutions to a problem. It gets the group to establish what key things are essential. It also allows them to place a weighting on the 'nice to have' issues, which have now become dispensable, enabling the group to move ahead with its work.

TIME BEAM

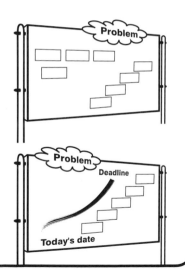

- Write the problem on the board and ask team
  members to brainstorm solutions. Each
  suggestion should be discussed and agreed
  with the team before being displayed
  (on cards/post-it notes).

- Get them to turn the board around and draw
  a diagonal line (see opposite) from top right
  (the deadline for problem solution) to bottom
  left (today's date). Ask them to rewrite each
  suggestion as an action step and to plot
  each step onto the time beam line at the
  appropriate 'date'.

PROBLEM-SOLVING/REFRAMING TECHNIQUES

EUREKA

This is a technique for solving a problem in an illogical way by making forced associations with totally unrelated pictures.

Before posing the problem to a group, pick three pictures at random and ask them to brainstorm the first word which comes to mind. Make three lists of words and then pose the problem.

Only ideas which are generated by **combining** one word from each list may be considered and then built on and elaborated into viable solutions.

65

PROBLEM-SOLVING/REFRAMING TECHNIQUES

NOTES

Note here other ideas which fit your own situation:

* _____

* _____

* _____

* _____

* _____

HELPFUL ATTITUDES
& VALUES

HELPFUL ATTITUDES & VALUES

MY MIND-SET WON'T HELP THEM

One of the principal errors facilitators make is that they impose their ideas on the group as they search for an answer to a particular problem. This is often because the facilitator has greater experience than the others in the group and perhaps has seen this specific situation many times in the past. The temptation is always there to try to get the group to see it your way.

In this case, the group miss out on the opportunity to discover their own way to the solution. They also lose the opportunity to discover a better way than that which is possible using the facilitator's frame of reference.

Facilitators must recognise that, in many instances, working with mature, experienced people requires that we put our own mind-sets into abeyance in order to remain neutral enough to help others.

UNCONDITIONAL POSITIVE REGARD

Facilitators draw knowledge from many other disciplines as they go about their work with groups and individuals. The counselling profession has always had a tradition of **unconditional positive regard** towards its clients, and it is an appropriate concept for facilitators' work also.

Unconditional positive regard means, briefly, that no matter what the client's personal attributes, views, appearance, behaviours, etc, the facilitator will always regard the individual as a human, unique and with enormous potential to be respected as such.

As you can imagine, this is a difficult aspiration given that so many of the people we meet can cause us discomfort, to say the least! Nevertheless, it is also vital that facilitators realise that they can't help their 'difficult' clients otherwise.

IT'S OK TO TEACH!

Some people think you should **always** facilitate; that process is **always** more important than content. Here's a modern-day parable for you to consider.

Vassili Tator is an earnest young training specialist with the United Nations in Geneva. Vassili has been taught that all human beings have unlimited potential and that the best way for people to learn is to share their knowledge with each other.

One summer Vassili set off to Papua New Guinea to teach an isolated tribe, who had survived happily for many millennia without electricity, how to use and maintain a gasoline-powered generator.

Having unpacked the crates of equipment and set up his flip charts, he gathered the scantily-clad, smiling natives around him. In well-rehearsed but halting phrases of local dialect he began:

"Now I want you to break into triads and discuss the steps you think we should take in order to complete a sound, regular maintenance of this generator. Please be ready to make a short presentation of your group's findings in 20 minutes from now."

NO ONE BEST WAY

Researchers into management behaviour have always sought the 'Holy Grail' of the one best way to manage people. More recently, however, we have come to accept that situational leadership and contingency approaches to management have real value in this diverse world. So we look for approaches which fit the situation rather than try to apply the 'one best way' to all circumstances.

There are two important lessons for facilitators here. Firstly, the principal idea behind having a facilitator work with the group is to generate a **custom-made** solution for that group and that situation. **Ready-made** solutions and answers, held by the facilitator, are probably inappropriate.

Secondly, facilitators should be open to changing the techniques and tools they themselves use when working with groups (especially when the group desires such changes). Simply adhering to the 'tried and trusted' ways of facilitating may be comfortable for the facilitator, but perhaps he or she is clinging on to tradition whilst exhorting the group to change and be flexible.

PEOPLE NEVER ARGUE WITH THEIR OWN DATA

Trainers have known this for years. Clever trainers always celebrate the data produced by the group and use it to help people to teach themselves. How many times have you seen experienced trainers post the output of group work onto the walls as 'trophies' for each group to admire? They cleverly invite experienced participants to help co-deliver parts of the course. They draw on the experience of the group in order to help them to see the value of their teaching and to prevent cognitive dissonance arising when new concepts are introduced.

It's the same for facilitators! The good ones know that the answers lie within the group and that their role is to help bring these answers out. They do this by getting the group, at all stages of the process, to understand that they own what is happening in the room and that they are the principal actors in the situation. So, every stage of the process is agreed and signed off before moving onto the next.

Before the facilitation begins, participants are encouraged to help define objectives; each individual's needs are established and recorded during the early stages of the process; participants themselves are involved in administration, such as writing up ideas and actions.

Good facilitators never get into arguments because people never argue with....

FACILITATORS CAN'T WIN ARGUMENTS

You can never win an argument with a customer! So the saying goes in good customer service texts, and the same applies in facilitation. Yet it's so tempting to engage with someone in a debate when we know exactly why and where they are wrong! If only they would just listen, see things our way, come to their senses, etc.

Skilled facilitators understand that such emotions and attitudes are counter-productive. They can empathise with someone who is being told by an 'expert' that they are wrong. They know that nobody likes being told they are wrong. Facilitators educate participants by understanding that education means 'to lead out'.

They do this by using open questions to help the challenger see the way forward: 'How would that work in practice?' 'What are the downsides to that idea?' 'What are the implications of your views?'

HELPFUL ATTITUDES & VALUES

SILENCE IS OK

In speeches and presentations a little silence can be a powerful tool for creating emphasis, or for getting audience attention. When silence lasts for longer than a few seconds in these instances, people get embarrassed. Try it yourself while chairing your next meeting and see how long it takes for someone to fill the silence with a comment or interjection, however useless it may be. We are uncomfortable with silences when it is our responsibility to present, chair or to facilitate.

Silence, however, is OK! There may be times during a facilitation when a person (or a group) has to take time to think about something important which has just happened and which needs consideration. As a facilitator your duty is to allow that to take place.

On other occasions you may have just asked a question about a sensitive issue which must be answered and dealt with by the group. Silence from you indicates that you intend to wait for the answer and that your questions are to be respected. Silence can also be used to allow an introverted group to process information internally. How much silence? Every situation is different but we would suggest that you move on after about 45 seconds!

DON'T PUSH THE RIVER

Don't push the river; it flows by itself! This is an old adage used by facilitators to indicate that you should not force a group towards a solution that they can't reach on their own.

Should facilitators pull or push? The answer seems to lie with the group.

Some facilitators will not go any further than a group wishes to initially. There are two dimensions to this. Facilitators can push a group to do more work, but they can also push a group to disclose more, and to go deeper into sensitive issues which are causing problems.

We take the view that the facilitator should push to do more work only if he/she feels there is the energy there to complete the task. In terms of disclosure and sensitive issues, the facilitator should push only as far as the group is willing to co-operate freely with the direction given.

The challenge for facilitators is that they can't push the river but they still have to make sure it gets to the sea!

NOTES

THE KNOWLEDGE BASE
Useful theories for facilitators

THE KNOWLEDGE BASE

LEARNING STYLES

Some people learn by trying something new and then thinking about it, and others by thinking first, then trying. There are four basic types of learner:

The Activist
- learns best by testing new knowledge or skills immediately and then correcting

The Reflector
- learns best by thinking carefully about how to apply new learning before acting

The Theorist
- learns best by conceptualising how the learning fits with coherent models and theories

The Pragmatist
- is highly practical; only learns if new knowledge makes sense and can help him/her achieve goals

Based on Honey & Mumford: 'Using your learning styles', 1986

THE KNOWLEDGE BASE

FOUR PHASES OF TEAM DEVELOPMENT

Form   During the start-up phase for a new team, members tentatively explore the boundaries of acceptable group behaviour. As the team forms, they want to establish themselves as participants and worry about being left out.

Storm   In the storming phase, members realise that the task is difficult and grow impatient with lack of progress. They argue about the actions the team should take, rely on their personal and professional experience, resist collaboration and become irritable and/or stubborn.

Norm   During the norming phase, members reconcile competing loyalties and responsibilities. They see the need to create rules and behavioural norms. Competitive relationships become more collaborative and the team members begin to work with each other.

Perform In the final, performing phase, team members discover each other's strengths and weaknesses, understand and accept their roles and work in synergy toward meeting their objectives.

Adapted from B.W. Tuckman: 'Developmental Sequence in Small Groups', 1965

THE KNOWLEDGE BASE

NLP

The basic premise of Neuro Linguistic Programming (NLP) is that people think about things by representing them in one of, or a mixture of, three ways:

Visually   - they see pictures

Auditorily   - they hear voice and sounds

Kinaesthetically - they feel emotions and sense things (touch, taste, smell)

Each person has a personal channel preference and, indeed, a personal strategy for processing information. Some of us prefer and use imagery in our speech and thoughts, others sense rather than see or hear, etc. People tend to programme themselves to think in certain ways, but this can be changed by helping them to represent things in a different way. With appropriate 'anchors' or reminders, the new ways of thinking can stick.

Trainers must be aware that participants will be processing information differently and, therefore, vary the channels on which they transmit information.

THE KNOWLEDGE BASE

DISSONANCE & SELF-JUSTIFICATION

When we are confronted with information
which contradicts a deeply-held view,
we suffer 'cognitive dissonance'.

We have two ways of dealing with this
dissonance:
1. **Change our opinion**
2. **Self-justify**
   - discredit the source of the information
   - distort the meaning of the information
     to fit our present view
   - seek alternative evidence to support
     our present view

Based on Elliot Aronson

THE KNOWLEDGE BASE

LOCUS OF CONTROL

The term 'locus of control' describes the way individuals attribute responsibility for events either to factors **within** themselves, or to factors **outside** their control. People who believe that control rests within themselves are referred to as **internals**. These people see themselves as being in control of their own lives. Those who believe that their lives are controlled by factors external to them, such as fate, luck and powerful people, are referred to as **externals**.

Internals are more likely to be mature, self-reliant, and responsible, to have greater levels of job satisfaction and prefer a participatory management style. Externals are less likely to be able to cope with the demands of reality. They often express unrealistic job aspirations. Internals exhibit far more self-direction and accept more responsibility for life events.

In debate, internals rely more on personal persuasion but externals use threats to win out. In choosing teams, internals are more likely to team up with those of equal or superior ability to themselves. Externals will choose people with inferior ability and delegate less.

Locus of control is a learned behaviour and it can be changed. Training programmes which bring an awareness of the current position and a knowledge of the process or mechanisms of change can be very successful.

UNFREEZE, MOVE, REFREEZE

This is a very simple procedure known as **unfreeze, move and refreeze**. Yet, despite its simplicity, it is not simplistic and requires diligent application.

Kurt Lewin proposed that in a change situation it was vital to:

- **Dissolve** the crystallisation of current behaviour using a series of techniques (unfreeze)

- **Transport** to a new level of operation the entire social system (move)

- **Secure** the new system against reverting to the old ways or to some other unintended result (refreeze).

Organisations using this approach start by recognising the need for change (unfreezing); then they mobilise commitment and energy around a purpose (moving); then they institutionalise the new order (refreezing). This is only one of Lewin's many major contributions to change literature.

THE BASES OF POWER

Power is the ability to influence the thoughts or actions of others. Power does not so much exist inherently in the person who has it, as in the minds of those who perceive that he has it.

French and Raven declare that power is not an entity in itself. It is the ability to influence others through five bases of power.

- **Coercive** power is exercised through punishment or threats and having control over some desired good which the other wants

- **Reward** power is being able to grant favours or benefits to someone

- **Referent** power is being attractive to another who wishes to please you

- **Expert** power is having a competence which is scarce

- **Legitimate** power is holding an office to which is attached certain rights

Informational and **connection** power have been added by recent writers to the above five bases.

ORGANISATIONAL DEVELOPMENT
A DEFINITION

> *"Growth can take place with or without development and vice versa. For example, a cemetery can grow without developing, so can a rubbish heap. A nation, corporation, or an individual can develop without growing ... development is an increase in capacity and potential, not an increase in attainment ... it has less to do with how much one has than with how much one can do with whatever one has."*
>
> ***(Ackoff, 1981)***

CULTURE

A DEFINITION

"*Basic assumptions and beliefs that are shared by members of an organisation, that operate unconsciously, and that define in a basic 'taken for granted' fashion an organisation's view of itself and its environment.*

These assumptions and beliefs are learned responses to a group's problems of internal integration. They come to be taken for granted because they solve those problems repeatedly and reliably.

This deeper level of assumptions is to be distinguished from the 'artefacts' and 'values' that are manifestations or surface levels of culture but not the essence of the culture."

(Schein, 1985)

SELF-FULFILLING PROPHECY

Whatever we dwell on expands in our minds and becomes self-reinforcing.

If we firmly believe that others are hostile to us then we are likely to behave in an unfriendly or even an aggressive manner. People who interact with us may be entirely neutral to begin with. However, they may perceive our behaviour in a negative light. They may even consider our behaviour as an unprovoked attack. In this case, they are likely to respond in a similar vein. Instantly, our initial preconceptions will be confirmed and will have become a self-fulfilling prophecy.

The answer is to realise that our subconscious cannot take a joke. The negative self-talk which goes on inside our heads minute by minute can be changed by our command to a positive self-fulfilling prophecy.

Facilitators must remain in full control by being aware of the power of the self-fulfilling prophecy, an antidote to the negative effects of which is to be found in 'Unconditional Positive Regard' on page 69.

REFERENCES & FURTHER READING

'Masterful Facilitation', A. Glenn Kisep, Amacom, 1998

'The Compleate Facilitator', Howick Associates, 1994

'The Trainer's Pocketbook', John Townsend, Management Pocketbooks, 1997

'The Learner's Pocketbook', Paul Hayden, Management Pocketbooks, 1995

'Using Your Learning Styles', Honey & Mumford, 1986

'NLP at Work', Sue Knight, NB Publishing, 1995

'Creating the Corporate Future', R.L. Ackoff, New York: Wiley, 1981

'The Social Animal', E. Aronson, New York: W.H. Freeman, 1995

'Organization Development – a Normative View', W.W. Burke, Reading, Ma: Addison-Wesley, 1987

REFERENCES & FURTHER READING

'Organisation Change and Development', M. Beer, Santa Monica, Calif: Goodyear, 1980

'OD and the Self Fulfilling Prophecy: Boosting Productivity by Raising Expectations', D. Eden, Journal of Applied Behavioural Science, 22(1), 1-13, 1986

'The Bases of Social Power', J.R.P. French & B. Raven, in D. Cartwright (Ed.), Studies in Social Power, Ann Arbor, MI: Institute for Social Research, The University of Michigan, 1959

'Gifts Differing', I.B. Myers & P.B. Myers, Palo Alto: Davies-Black, 1995

'Organizational Culture and Leadership', E.H. Schein, San Francisco: Jossey Bass, 1985

'Psychological Bulletin', B.W. Tuckman, Developmental Science in Small Groups 63, 384-399, 1965

About the Author

John Townsend, BA MA MCIPD
John is the founder of the Master Trainer Institute.
He founded the Institute after 30 years of experience in
international consulting and human resource management
positions in the UK, France, the United States and Switzerland.

From 1978-1984 he was European Director of Executive
Development with GTE in Geneva with training
responsibility for over 800 managers in some 15 countries.
John has published a number of management and professional
guides and regularly contributes articles to leading management and
training journals.

In addition to training trainers, he is also a regular speaker at conferences and leadership
seminars throughout Europe.

Contact
Courses based on this pocketbook are run at:
The Master Trainer Institute, L'Avant Centre, 13 chemin du Levant, Ferney-Voltaire, France.
Tel: (33) 450 42 84 16   Fax: (33) 450 40 57 37   www.mt-institute.com

About the Author

Paul Donovan MSc (Mgmt.)

Paul is Head of Programmes with the Irish Management Institute in Dublin where he is responsible for a suite of training and development programmes for HRD professionals. He has extensive management experience and has conducted a wide range of HRD assignments in Western Europe and Asia.

Paul's professional interests include researching evaluation of training and development interventions where he has identified easy-to-use surrogate measures as effective replacements for time-consuming and expensive evaluation initiatives. He has edited seven books in a series of management texts.

Contact

Paul Donovan can be contacted at: Irish Management Institute, Sandyford, Dublin 16, Ireland.
Tel: 353 1 2078474   E-mail: donovanp@imi.ie

Published by:
Management Pocketbooks Ltd
Laurel House, Station Approach, Alresford, Hants SO24 9JH, U.K.
Tel: +44 (0)1962 735573   Fax: +44 (0)1962 733637
E-mail: sales@pocketbook.co.uk
Website: www.pocketbook.co.uk

This edition published 1999   Reprinted 2000, 2001, 2002, 2003, 2004, 2005, 2007.

© John Townsend & Paul Donovan 1999

ISBN   978 1 870471 70 1

British Library Cataloguing-in-Publication Data – A catalogue record for this book is available from the British Library.

Design, typesetting and graphics by **efex Ltd.**   Printed in U.K.

THE MANAGEMENT POCKETBOOK SERIES

Pocketbooks

Appraisals
Assertiveness
Balance Sheet
Business Planning
Business Writing
Call Centre Customer Care
Career Transition
Challengers
Coaching
Communicator's
Competencies
Controlling Absenteeism
Creative Manager's
C.R.M.
Cross-cultural Business
Cultural Gaffes
Customer Service
Decision-making
Developing People
Discipline
Diversity
E-commerce
Emotional Intelligence
Employment Law
Empowerment

Energy and Well-being
Facilitator's
Flexible Workplace
Handling Complaints
Icebreakers
Impact & Presence
Improving Efficiency
Improving Profitability
Induction
Influencing
International Trade
Interviewer's
I.T. Trainer's
Key Account Manager's
Leadership
Learner's
Manager's
Managing Budgets
Managing Cashflow
Managing Change
Managing Recruitment
Managing Upwards
Managing Your Appraisal
Marketing
Meetings

Mentoring
Motivation
Negotiator's
Networking
NLP
Openers & Closers
People Manager's
Performance Management
Personal Success
Positive Mental Attitude
Presentations
Problem Behaviour
Problem Solving
Project Management
Quality
Resolving Conflict
Sales Excellence
Salesperson's
Self-managed Development
Starting In Management
Strategy
Stress
Succeeding at Interviews
Teambuilding Activities
Teamworking

Telephone Skills
Telesales
Thinker's
Time Management
Trainer Standards
Trainer's
Training Evaluation
Training Needs Analysis
Virtual Teams
Vocal Skills

Pocketsquares

Great Training Robbery
Hook Your Audience

Pocketfiles

Trainer's Blue Pocketfile of
Ready-to-use Activities

Trainer's Green Pocketfile of
Ready-to-use Activities

Trainer's Red Pocketfile of
Ready-to-use Activities

27.2.06

ORDER FORM

Handwritten: M1082816 09/10/07
Handwritten: 048685 658.312470w

Your details

Name _____

Position _____

Company _____

Address _____

_____

Telephone _____

Fax _____

E-mail _____

VAT No. (EC companies) _____

Your Order Ref _____

Please send me: *6.99*

The _Facilitator's_ Pocketbook ☐ No. copies

The _____ Pocketbook ☐

The _____ Pocketbook ☐

The _____ Pocketbook ☐

The _____ Pocketbook ☐

Order by Post

MANAGEMENT POCKETBOOKS LTD

LAUREL HOUSE, STATION APPROACH,
ALRESFORD, HAMPSHIRE SO24 9JH UK

Order by Phone, Fax or Internet

Telephone: +44 (0)1962 735573
Facsimile: +44 (0)1962 733637
E-mail: sales@pocketbook.co.uk
Web: www.pocketbook.co.uk